SHAKESPEARE

A LAWYER

BY

WILLIAM L. RUSHTON

THE LAWBOOK EXCHANGE, LTD.
Clark, New Jersey
2006

ISBN-13: 978-1-58477-699-4
ISBN-10: 1-58477-699-4

Second printing 2009

The quality of this reprint is equivalent to the quality of the original work.

Printed in the United States of America on acid-free paper

THE LAWBOOK EXCHANGE, LTD.
33 Terminal Avenue
Clark, New Jersey 07066-1321

Please see our website for a selection of our other publications and fine facsimile reprints of classic works of legal history:
www.lawbookexchange.com

Library of Congress Cataloging-in-Publication Data

Rushton, William Lowes.
Shakespeare a lawyer / William L. Rushton.
p. cm.
Originally published: London, England : Longman, Brown, Green, Longman, and Roberts, 1858.
ISBN-13: 978-1-58477-699-4 (alk. paper)
ISBN-10: 1-58477-699-4 (alk. paper)
1. Shakespeare, William, 1564-1616--Knowledge--Law. 2. Law and literature--History--16th century. 3. Law and literature--History--17th century. 4. Law--Great Britain--History--16th century.
5. Law--Great Britain--History--17th century. 6. Lawyers in literature. 7. Law in literature. I. Title.
PR3028R77 2006
822.3'3--dc22 2006002536

SHAKESPEARE

A LAWYER

BY

WILLIAM L. RUSHTON

LONDON
LONGMAN BROWN GREEN LONGMANS AND ROBERTS

LIVERPOOL
WEBB AND HUNT CASTLE-STREET

MDCCCLVIII

SHAKESPEARE A LAWYER.

"Sometime like a lawyer."
Timon of Athens.

"And still they gazed, and still the wonder grew,
That one small head could carry all he knew."
Goldsmith.

Τῆς φύσεως γραμματεὺς ἦν, τὸν κάλαμον ἀποβρέχων εἰς νοῦν.
Suidas.

THE works of William Shakespeare contain a remarkable quantity of law terms, whose significations are naturally unknown to the generality of readers. Some of the admirers of our great dramatist may assert that the universality of his genius, the strength, vigour, and magnitude of his intellectual faculties and powers of investigation, enabled him to acquire a more profound knowledge of a greater variety of subjects than ever yet seems to have been possessed by the same individual, and that the legal knowledge he has displayed in the *correct* use of law terms is not more remarkable than his intimate acquaintance with human nature, and accurate observation of the habits and customs of mankind, or than the knowledge of seamanship, and the correct use of nautical terms he has displayed in the *Tempest*. To attempt to account for the frequent occurrence and correct use of law terms in

Shakespeare's Works, by attributing to him unusual knowledge of a great variety of subjects, is not satisfactory; for, Shakespeare's knowledge, it is generally admitted, was more intuitive than acquired, consisting more in an extensive and profound intimacy with human nature, with the animal and inanimate world,—which he has displayed with a truthfulness, power, and sublimity unapproached, if not unapproachable, rather than in a familiarity with the writings of authors and science in general,—and if that master mind could possibly have possessed double the unequalled genius which exalted him far above the generality of his fellow creatures, he would not have been able to use and apply law terms of a purely technical character in the manner appearing in his compositions, without considerable knowledge of that abstruse and mighty science, the law of England. Nor will it be satisfactory to state that the legal knowledge he has displayed in the correct use of law terms affords no more evidence of his having been a lawyer than the correct use of nautical terms and the knowledge of seamanship affords of his having been sometime a seaman,—because the sea phrases and the display of knowledge of seamanship are peculiar to the *Tempest*,—those phrases are not of frequent occurrence, and that knowledge is not displayed in any other portion of his works. Morever, if it can be proved, as there seems reason to believe, that the principles and practice of the law of real property were more generally understood by unprofessional people in Shakespeare's time than at the present day, that circumstance will not satisfactorily account for all Shakespeare's legal knowledge, because his works contain passages displaying not merely a knowledge of the principles and practice of the law of real property, but also of the common law, and of the criminal law, and a thorough intimacy with the exact letter of the Statute Law.

SUFFOLK. "Lord Cardinal, the King's further pleasure is,
Because all those things you have done of late
By your power legatine within this kingdom,
Fall into the compass of a *præmunire*,—
That, therefore, such a writ be sued against you,
To forfeit all your *goods*, *lands*, *tenements*,
Chattels, and whatsoever, and to be
Out of the King's protection. This is my charge."

Henry VIII., Act 3, Scene 2.

A *Præmunire* (so called from the words of the writ Præmunire facias, or Præmoneri facias, signifying the writ and the offence on which the writ is grounded) is an offence whereby one shall incur the same punishment which is inflicted upon those who transgress the 16th Richard II., chap. 5, commonly called the Statute of Præmunire, which enacts that "If any purchase or pursue, or cause to be purchased or pursued in the Court of Rome, or elsewhere, any translation, process, sentence of excommunication, bulls, instruments, &c., which touch the King; or if any do bring them within the realm, or receive them, they shall *be put out of the King's protection*, and their *lands, tenements, goods and chattels, forfeited to the King*." (See the exposition of this statute, 3rd Inst., 126, and see 28th Henry VIII., chap. 16, which is a general law, and strictly penned against pleading any bull, dispensation, &c., from Rome, which is not warranted by the act. Wood's Institute, 2nd ed., p. 408.) This offence originated from the power claimed and exercised by the Pope, which even in the days of blind zeal was too exorbitant for our ancestors to endure.

DUKE. "Whoe'er he be, that in this foul proceeding,
Hath thus beguiled your daughter of herself,
And you of her, the bloody book of law
You shall read in the bitter *letter*,
After your own sense; yea, though our proper son
Stood in your action.

OTHELLO. I will a round unvarnish'd tale deliver
Of my whole course of love; what *drugs*, what charms,
What *conjuration*, and what mighty magic,
(For such proceeding I am charged withal,)
I won his daughter with."

The 8th cap. 33rd Henry VIII., against conjurations, witchcraft, sorceries, and enchantments, enacts "It shall be felony to practice, or cause to be practised, *conjuration*, witchcraft, enchantment, or sorcery, to get money; or to consume any person in his body, members, or goods; or *to provoke any person to unlawful love*; or for despight of Christ, or lucre of money, to pull down any cross; or to declare where goods stolen be." (See also 5th Eliz., cap. 5.) These passages sufficiently prove that Shakespeare's knowledge of the English law was not confined to the *lex non scripta*, for he uses almost the exact language of the statutes. It may, however, be asserted that probably chance made Shakespeare familiar with law terms; but chance would not have enabled him to apply them with such correctness. Moreover, why should Shakespeare make use of law terms in preference to the technical terms of the medical, clerical, or any other profession? It will also be perceived, in the passages about to be selected, that the great dramatist, in addition to a frequent use of law terms and law phraseology, makes constant reference to lawyers in his allusions to mankind, in apparent preference to the members of any other profession. Why should *Hamlet*, in his reflections on a skull, suppose that it belonged to a lawyer, in preference to a doctor or a divine? But let the reader notice how many law terms are made use of in this passage:

HAMLET. "Why may not that be the skull of a lawyer? Where be his *quiddets* now, his *quillets*, his *cases*, his *tenures*, and his tricks? Why does he suffer this rude knave now to knock him about the sconce with a dirty shovel, and will not tell him of his *action of battery*? This fellow might be in 's time a buyer of land, with his *statutes*, his *recognizances*, his *fines*, his *double* vouchers, his *recoveries*. Is this the *fine* of his *fines*, and the *recovery* of his *recoveries*, to have his *fine* pate full of *fine* dirt? Will his *vouchers* vouch him no more of his *purchases*, and *double* ones too, than the length and breadth of a pair of *indentures*? The very conveyance of his lands will hardly lie in this *box*, and must the inheritor himself have no more?"

Quiddets and *quillets*, *cases* and *tenures*, are terms with which many persons, who are not at all familiar with the laws of England, are perfectly well acquainted. But *statutes* and *recognizances*, *fines*, *double vouchers*, and *recoveries* are somewhat more technical and abstruse. Recognizance, *(recognitio,)* though in special signification it only acknowledges a certain debt, and is executed upon all the goods and half of the lands of the recognisor, yet by extension it is drawn also to *bonds*, commonly called *statute* merchant and *statute* of the staple. A statute merchant (so called from the 13th Edward I., De mercatoribus,) was a *bond* acknowledged before one of the clerks of the statutes merchant, and mayor, or chief warden of the city of London, or two merchants of the said city, for that purpose assigned; or before the mayor, chief warden, or master of other cities or good towns, or other sufficient men for that purpose appointed, sealed with the seal of the depter and of the King, which was of two pieces, the greater was kept by the said mayor, chief warden, &c., and the lesser piece thereof by the said clerks. Statute staple was either properly so called, or improperly. A *statute staple*, properly so called, was a *bond* of record, acknowledged before the mayor of the staple, in the presence of the two constables of the same staple, founded upon the statute anno 27th Edward III., cap. 9. A statute staple improper, was a bond of record, founded upon the statute anno 23rd Henry VIII., cap. 6, of the nature of a proper statute staple, as touching the forces and execution thereof, and acknowledged before one of the chief justices, and, in their absence, before the mayor of the staple and the recorder of London. The *statutes* referred to by *Hamlet* are doubtless *statutes merchant* and *statutes staple*, and not acts of parliament; because between these *statutes* and recognizances there exists a reciprocal relation. Statutes staple, statutes merchant, and recognizances, in the nature of a statute staple, are now obsolete. The term *fine*, as used by Shakespeare in this passage, signified an amicable agreement or composition of a suit, whether real or fictitious, between the demandant and tenant, with the consent of the judges, and enrolled among the records of the court where the suit was commenced, by which lands and tenements were transferred from one person to another, or any other settlement was made respecting them. This assurance was called *finis*, or *finalis concordia*, from the words with which it began, and also from its effect, which was to put an *end* to all suits and contentions. Thus, Glanville says: "Et nota quod dicitur talis concordia finalis, eo quod finem imponit negotio, adeo ut neuter ligitantium ab eâ de cetera poterit recedere;" and Bracton says: "Finis est extremitas unius cujusque rei, et ideo dicitur finalis concordia, quia imponit finem litibus." A *recovery*, in its most extensive sense, was a restoration of a former right, by the solemn judgment of a court of justice; and judgment, whether obtained after a real defence made by the tenant, or upon his default, or feint plea, had the same force and efficacy to bind the right of the land so recovered, and to vest a free and absolute estate in fee-simple in the recoveror. A common recovery was a judgment obtained in a fictitious suit, brought against the tenant of the freehold in consequence of a default made by the person who was last vouched to warranty in such suit. The end and effect of this recovery was to discontinue and destroy estates tail, remainders, and reversions, and to bar the former owners thereof, and in this formality three parties were required, namely, the defendant, he that brought the writ of entry, and might be termed the recoveror; the tenant, he against whom the writ was brought, and might be termed the recoveree; and the vouchee, he whom the tenant vouched, or called to warranty for the land in demand.

PASANIO. "Here 's a *voucher*
Stronger than ever law could make."

Cymbeline, Act 2, Scene 2.

CORIOLANUS. "Why in this wolfish gown should I stand here,
To beg of Hob and Dick, that do appear,
Their needless *vouches*? Custom calls me to 't."

Act 2, Scene 3.

A recovery might be, and was, frequently suffered with *double*, treble, or further voucher, as the exigency of the case required, in which case there were several judgments against the several vouchees.

The reader will from this explanation perceive that Shakespeare has used the terms *recovery* and *double voucher* not indiscriminately, but in a relative sense, as the mention of one term suggests the idea of the other, with which it is inseparably connected. Fines and recoveries were abolished by the 3rd and 4th William IV., c. 74, which contains provisions enabling tenants in tail to dispose of their estate so as to create a fee-simple absolute, or any less estate. This act received the royal assent on the 28th August, 1833, and came into operation on the 1st January, 1834.

Shakespeare displays his acquaintance with the custom of conveyancing lawyers in this passage:

> "The very conveyance of his lands will hardly lie in this box; and must the inheritor himself have no more?"

Why should *Hamlet* compare the grave to a box? Not because there is any resemblance between a box and a grave, but because conveyancers and attorneys keep their deeds in wood or tin boxes. If the reader, recollecting the explanations that have been made, will take the trouble to dwell a short time on these reflections of *Hamlet*, he will perceive that the word *fine* there made use of is intended to signify, not a penalty, but an end. The *fine* of his *fines* means the end or termination of his fines. That his fine pate is filled, not with fine dirt, but with the *last* dirt which will ever occupy it, leaving a satirical inference to be drawn, that even in his lifetime his head was filled with dirt. From the following passages it appears that Shakespeare uses the term *fine* in that sense:

HELENA. "All's well that ends well: still the *fine*'s the crown;
Whate'er the course, the *end* is the renown."

All's Well That Ends Well, Act 4, Scene 4.

BENEDICT. "And the *fine* is (for the which I may go the finer) I will live a bachelor."

Much Ado About Nothing, Act 1, Scene 1.

"Time's office is to *fine* the hate of foes;
To eat up errors by opinion bred,
Not spend the dowry of a lawful bed."

The Rape of Lucrece.

IAGO. "Poor and content, is rich and rich enough;
But riches *fineless* is as poor as winter
To him that fears he shall be poor."

Othello, Act 3, Scene 3.

MRS. PAGE. "The spirit of wantonness is sure scared out of him; if the devil have him not *in fee-simple, with fine and recovery,* he will never, I think, in the way of waste, attempt us again."

Merry Wives of Windsor, Act 4, Scene 2.

Tenant in fee-simple, in the language of Littleton, is he which hath lands or tenements to hold to him and to his heirs for ever. And it is called, in Latin, *feodum simplex*, for *feodum* is the same that inheritance is, and *simplex* is as much to say lawful or pure; and so *feodum simplex* signifies a lawful or pure inheritance; and *fine* and *recovery* was formerly the strongest assurance known to the English law.

"Non in regno Angliæ providetur vel est aliqua securitas major seu solennior per quam aliquis vel aliqua statum certiorem habere possit, vel ad statum suam verificandum aliquod solennius testimonium producere, quam finem in curia domini regis levatum; qui quidem finis sic vocatur, eo finis et consummatio omnium placitorum esse debet; et quod hoc de causâ providebatur.—2 *Roll Ab.* 13, 18*th Edward I.*

Mrs. Page means to say that the devil had as absolute power over Falstaff as a man has over an inheritance of which he is seized in fee-simple in possession.

CADE. "Here 's the lord of the soil come to seize me for a *stray*, entering his *fee-simple* without leave."

Henry VI., Act 4, *Scene* 10.

"Stray, Estrays *(Estrahuræ)* are cattle that stray into another man's ground and not own'd by any man. In this case, if they are proclaimed on two market days in two several towns next adjoining, and the owner doth not claim them within a year and a day, they belong to the Lord of the Liberty."—*Finch*, 177; *Kitch*, 80, 81; *Bacon Elem*, 76, 77; *Wood's Institute, 2d edition, p.* 213.

"My woeful self, that did in freedom stand,
And was my own *fee-simple*, (not in part,)
What with his art in youth, and youth in art,
Threw my affections in his charmed power,
Reserved the stalk, and gave him all my flower."

A Lover's Complaint.

DROMIO OF SYRACUSE. "There 's no time for a man to recover his hair that grows bald by nature.

ANTIPHOLUS OF SYRACUSE. "May he not do it by *fine and recovery?*

DRO. S. "Yes, to pay a fine for a peruke, and recover the lost hair of another man."

Comedy of Errors, Act 2, *Scene* 2.

THERSITES. "Incurable boneache, and the rivelled *fee-simple* of the tetter."

Troilus and Cressida, Act 5, *Scene* 1.

BENVOLIO. "An I were so apt to quarrel as thou art, any man should buy the *fee-simple* of my life for an hour and a quarter.

MERCUTIO. "The *fee-simple?* O simple."

Romeo and Juliet, Act 3, *Scene* 1.

PAROLLES. "For a quart d'écu he will sell the *fee-simple* of his salvation, the inheritance of it; and cut the *entail* from all *remainders*, and a perpetual succession for it perpetually."

All's Well That Ends Well, Act 4, Scene 3.

An estate in fee-tail (from *tailler*, to cut or limit) is that inheritance whereof one is seized to him and the heirs of his body, begotten or to be begotten.—*Litt, s.* 18; *Wood's Institute, 2nd edition, p.* 120.

An estate in remainder is the residue of an estate, in land, depending upon a particular estate, and created together with the same. A particular estate is that which is derived from a general and greater estate.—*Wood's Institute, 2nd edition, p.* 149.

The difference between a remainder and a reversion is, that a remainder is something limited over to a third person on the creation of an estate less than that which the grantor has; whilst a reversion is that part which remains in the grantor himself, on such a grant of a less estate.—*Co. Litt,* 22 *b.*; *Watk's Prin. Conv., ch.* 18; *Burton's Comp., pp.* 28, 29, 30; *Noy's Dial, p.* 13.

QUEEN. "'Tis in *reversion* that I do possess."

Richard II., Act 2, Scene 2.

KING RICHARD. "As were our England in *reversion* his,
And he our subject's next degree in hope."

Act 1, Scene 4.

DOUGLAS. "Where now remains a sweet *reversion*:
We may boldly spend upon the hope of what
Is to come in:
A comfort of retirement lives in this."

First Part Henry IV., Act 4, Scene 2.

TROILUS. "No perfect in *reversion* shall have a praise in present; we will not name desert, before his birth, and, being born, his *addition* shall be humble."

Troilus and Cressida, Act 3, Scene 2.

An estate in reversion (from *reverto*, to return) is where any estate is derived, by grant or otherwise, out of a larger one, leaving in the original owner an ulterior estate immediately expectant on that which is so derived; the latter interest is called the *particular estate*, (that is only a small part or *particula* of the original one,) and the ulterior interest the *reversion*.

STEWARD. "One whom I will beat into clamorous whining, if thou deny'st the least syllable of thy *addition*."

King Lear, Act 2, Scene 2.

HAMLET. "They clepe us, drunkards, and with swinish phrase
Soil our *addition*."

Hamlet, Act 1, Scene 4.

ALEXANDER. "This man, lady, hath robbed many beasts of their particular *additions*."

Troilus and Cressida, Act 1, Scene 2.

ULYSSES. "Bull-bearing Milo his *addition* yield,
To sinewy Ajax."

Troilus and Cressida, Act 2, Scene 3.

AJAX. "A great *addition* earned in thy death."

Troilus and Cressida, Act 4, Scene 5.

LEAR. "Only we still retain
The name and all the *additions* to a king."

The description of an individual in a legal document, as esquire, gentleman, yeoman, &c., is called his *addition*.

CADE. "Thou hast appointed justices of the peace, to call poor men before them about matters they were not able to answer. Moreover, thou hast put them in prison; and *because they could not read, thou hast hanged them*: when, indeed, only for that cause they have been most worthy to live."

Second Part Henry VI., Act 4, Scene 7.

In the days of Jack Cade few could read, except those who were actually in orders, or educated for that purpose:

[SMITH. "The Clerk of Chatham: he can write and read, and cast accompt."

CADE. "O monstrous!

SMITH. "We took him setting of boys' copies.

CADE. "Here's a villain!

SMITH. "H'as a book in his pocket, with red letters in't.

CADE. "Nay, then, he is a conjurer.

DICK. "Nay, he can make *obligations*, and write court-hand.

CADE. "Dost thou use to write thy name? or hast thou a mark to thyself, like an honest, plain dealing man?

CLERK. "Sir, I thank God, I have been so well brought up that I can write my name."

Second Part Henry VI., Act 4, Scene 2.]

so that if a person was arraigned before a temporal judge for any crime (the punishment whereof was death) he might pray his clergy; that was, to have a Latin Bible in a black Gothic character delivered to him; and if he could read a passage where the judge appointed, which was generally in the Psalms, the ordinary, or his deputy, who stood near, said, *legit ut clericus*, that is, he could read like a clerk or scholar, and the criminal was acquitted as being a man of learning, who might therefore be useful to the public; if, however, he could not read, he suffered death. This privilege was granted in all offences, except high treason and sacrilege, until after the year 1530; and it was carried to such an extent, that if a criminal was condemned at one assize, because he could not read, and was reprieved to the subsequent assize, he might again claim this benefit, either at that time, or even under the gallow's tree, and if he could then read, he was pardoned, of which there was an instance in the reign of Queen Elizabeth.

Although this privilege was originally enjoyed only by those who had the *habitum et tonsuram clericalem*, who wore the clerical habit and were trimmed with the clerical tonsure; yet the ability to read being formerly a mark of great erudition, every one thus qualified, in course of time, was considered a clerk, or *clericus*, and allowed the benefit of clergy, although not in holy orders. So that, ultimately, as many laymen as clergymen enjoyed this privilege, which excited the jealousy of the clergy, in whose favour, therefore, a further distinction was made, by stat. 4th Henry VII., chap. 13, in the year 1487, "*Whereas upon trust of the privilege of the church, divers persons lettered have been the more bold to commit murder, rape, robbery, theft, and all other mischievious deeds, because they have been continually admitted to the benefit of the clergy as oft as they did offend in any of the premises;* it is enacted, ordained, and established, by the authority of this present parliament, that every person, not being within orders, which once hath been admitted to the benefit of his clergy, eftsoons arraigned of any such offence, be not admitted to have the benefit or privilege of his clergy; and that every person so convicted for murder, to be marked with an M upon the braun of the left thumb; and if he be for any other felony, the same person to be marked with a T in the same place of the thumb, and those marks to be made by the gaoler openly in the court before the judge, before that such person be delivered to the ordinary."

DICK. "But, methinks, he should stand in fear of fire, being burnt i' the hand for stealing of sheep."

Second Part Henry VI., Act 4, Scene 2.

Hence, probably, the origin of the request made even at the present time, when a prisoner is arraigned, "Prisoner at the bar, hold up your hand," in order, if he was a layman, that it might thereby be ascertained whether he had been admitted to this privilege before. The benefit of clergy first legally recognised by stat. 3rd Edward I., A.D. 1274, modified in 1530, in the time of Henry VIII., was wholly repealed by the 7th and 8th Geo. IV., June, 1827.

MORTIMER. "And our *indentures tripartite* are drawn,
Which being *sealed interchangeably*," &c.

First Part Henry IV., Act 3, *Scene* 1.

A deed indented consists of two or more parts: for there are deeds Bipartite, of two parts; Tripartite, of three: Quadrupartite, of four; Quinquepartite, of five; and Sextipartite, of six, &c. In which respective deeds it is expressed, that the parties thereunto have *interchangeably set their hands and seals*.

PANDARUS. "Words pay no debts, give her deeds; but she'll bereave you of the deeds, too, if she call your activity in question. What, billing again? Here's IN WITNESS WHEREOF THE PARTIES INTERCHANGEABLY."

Troilus and Cressida, Act 3, *Scene* 1.

An indenture is so called because each part used formerly to be cut or indented in acute angles (instar dentium, or like the teeth of a saw) on the top, or side, to tally or correspond with the other.—(*Vide* Co. Litt., 47 b.; Litt., s. 371.) The history of the practice of indenting is given in Co. Litt., by Butler, 269, A.N. (1.) Formerly, when deeds were more concise than at present, it was usual to write both parts on the same piece of parchment, with same word or letters of the alphabet written between them, through which the parchment was cut, either in a straight or indented line, so as to leave half the word on one part and half on the other. But for a long time past the practice of cutting through any letters has, in all other instances, been disused; and even of indenting saw-wise, the modern method being to cut the top of the parchment in a waving line. Neither this, however, nor any other method of indenting is in general necessary to the legal validity of the instrument.

AUSTRIA. "Upon thy cheek I lay this zealous kiss,
As seal to this *indenture* of my love."

King John, Act 2, *Scene* 1.

"Let him but copy what in you is writ,
Not making worse what nature made so clear,
And such a *counterpart* shall fame his wit,
Making his style admired everywhere."

Sonnet lxxxiv.

When the several parts of an indenture are *interchangeably* executed by the several parties, that part or copy which is executed by the grantor is usually called the *original*, and the rest are *counterparts;* though, of late, it is most frequent for all the parties to execute every part, which renders them all originals.

ROSALIND. "With *bills* on their necks, —*Be it known unto all men by these presents.*"

As You Like It, Act 1, *Scene* 2.

The bills *Rosalind* mentions are deeds poll, which commonly begin *Know all men by these presents*, or *To all whom these presents shall come*, and are made by one party only, and not indented, but polled or shaved quite even, and therefore called a *deed poll*, or single deed.—*Mirror*, c. 2, *s.* 27; *Litt.*, *s.* 371, 372; *Gardner v. Lachlan.*

SLENDER. "A gentleman born master parson, who writes himself *armigero;* in a *bill*, warrant, quittance, or *obligation*, armigero."

An obligation, according to our common law, is a bond containing a penalty, with a condition for payment of money; or to do or suffer some act or thing, &c. If it is without condition, it is called a *bill*, which is sometimes with a penalty, and then it is called a penal *bill*, or simple bond. (1 Inst., 172a; 3 Cro., 515; 2 Roll, abr., 146; Wood's Institute, 2nd ed., p. 288.)

An obligation, or *bond*, is a deed whereby the obligor obliges himself, his heirs, executors, or administrators, to pay a certain sum of money to another at a day appointed. If this be all, the bond is a single one, *simplex obligatio*.

SHYLOCK. "Go with me to a notary, seal me there
Your *single bond*."

But a condition is generally added, that if the obligor does some particular act, the obligation shall be void, as performance of convenants, or repayment of a principal sum borrowed of the obligee, with interest, *which sum is usually one-half of the penal sum named in the bond.*

"Say for non-payment that the debt should *double*."
Venus and Adonis.

PORTIA. "What sum owes he the Jew?"
BASSANIO. "For me, *three* thousand ducats."
PORTIA. "What, no more!
Pay him *six* thousand and deface the bond."
Merchant of Venice, Act 3, Scene 4.

Bonds, with conditions of this kind annexed, have been long in use, and in former times on a conditional bond becoming forfeited for non-payment of the money borrowed, the *whole* penalty, usually double the principal sum lent by the obligee, was recoverable. (Litt. S. 40.) So *Macbeth* says:

"But yet I'll make assurance *double* sure,
And take a *bond* of fate."
Act 4, Scene 1.

Referring not to a single, but to a conditional bond, under or by virtue of which, when forfeited, double the principal sum was recoverable.

"Your accent is somewhat finer than you could *purchase* in so removed a dwelling." *As You Like It, Act 3, Scene 2.*

"For what in me was *purchased*
Falls upon thee in a much fairer sort."
Henry IV., Part 2.

OCTAVIUS CÆSAR. "A man, who is the abstract of all faults,
That all men follow.

LEPIDUS. "I must not think there are
Evils enough to darken all his goodness;
His faults, in him, seem as the spots of heaven,
More fiery by night's blackness—*hereditary*
Rather than *purchased.*"

Antony and Cleopatra, Act 1, Scene 4.

Purchase (perquisitio) has in law a meaning more extended than its ordinary signification. It is possession to which a man cometh not by title of descent. (Litt., s. 12.) It is contradistinguished from acquisition by right of blood, and includes every other method of coming to an estate whatever, than that by inheritance, wherein the title is vested in a person by single operation of the law. (1 Inst. 18.) Accordingly, a devisee under a will is now a purchaser in law. In these passages the word purchase is used by Shakespeare in its strict legal sense, in contradistinction to an acquisition by descent, although purchase was, in Shakespeare's days, sometimes used to signify robbery, and also the thing stolen:

"They will steal anything and call it *purchase.*"
Twelfth Night, Act 4, Scene 1.

PETRUCHIO. "What *dower* shall I have with her to wife?

BAPTISTA. "After my death, the one-half of my lands;
And, in possession, twenty thousand crowns.

PETRUCHIO. "And, for that *dowry*, I'll assure her of
Her widowhood,—be it that she survive me,—
In all my *lands* and *leases* whatsoever:
Let *specialties* be, therefore, drawn between us,
That *covenants* may be kept on either hand."

Taming the Shrew, Act 2, *Scene* 1.

"Tenant in dower is where a man is seized of lands or tenements in fee-simple, fee-tail general, or as heir in special tail, and taketh a wife, and dieth; the wife, after the decease of her husband, shall be endowed of the third part of such lands and tenements as were her husband's at any time during the coverture, to have and to hold to the same wife in severalty, by metes and bounds, for term of her life, whether she hath issue by her husband or no, and of what age soever the wife be, so as she be past the age of nine years at the time of the death of her husband, otherwise she shall not be endowed," (Litt. s. 36.) "And note, that by the common law the wife shall have for her dower but the third part of the tenements which were her husband's during the espousals; but, by the custom of some county, she shall have the half, and, by the custom in some town or borough, she shall have the whole; and in all these cases she shall be called tenant in dower," (Litt. s. 37.) Widowhood, a term only used now as descriptive of the state of being a widow, signified the estate settled on a widow. Petruchio says he will assure Katharina of a widow's portion in all his "lands and leases," and not "bar dower" by fine and recovery. "Also, there be two other kinds of dower, viz., dower which is called *dowment at the church door*, and dower called *dowment by the father's assent*."—Litt. s. 38.

BION. "His daughter is to be brought by you to supper.
LUCENTIO. "And then?

BION. "The old priest at Saint Luke's Church is at your command at all hours.

LUCENTIO. "And what of all this?

BION. "I cannot tell, except they are busied about counterfeit assurance. Take your assurance of her, *cum privilegio ad imprimendum solùm,* to the church; take the priest, clerk, and some sufficient honest witnesses."

Taming of the Shrew, Act 4, Scene 4.

Dowment at the church door *(dower ad ostium ecclesiæ)* is where a man of full age seized in fee-simple, who shall be married to a woman, and when he cometh to the church door to be married, there, after affiance and troth plighted between them, he endoweth the woman of his whole land, o of the half, or other lesser part thereof, and there openly doth declare the quantity and the certainty of the land which she shall have for her dower. In this case the wife, after the death of the husband, may enter into the said quantity of land of which her husband endowed her without other assignment of any.—Litt. s. 39.

BAPTISTA. "I must confess your offer is the best;
And let your father make her the assurance,
She is your own; else you must pardon me:
If you should die before him, where 's her *dower?*"

Taming of the Shrew, Act 2, Scene 1.

Baptista seems to refer to dowment by the father's assent, *(dower ex assensu patris,)* which is where the father is seized of tenements in fee, and his son and heir apparent, when he is married, endoweth his wife at the monastery or church door, of parcel of his father's lands or tenements with the assent of his father, and assigns the quantity and parcels. In this case, after the death of the son, the wife shall enter into the same parcel without the assignment of any.—Litt. s. 40.

"O, brother Montague, give me thy hand; this my daughter's *jointure*, for no more can I demand." *Romeo and Juliet.*

A jointure is thus defined by Sir Edward Coke:—"A competent livelihood of freehold for the wife, of lands and tenements, to take effect presently, in possession or profit, after the decease of the husband, for the life of the wife at least." This description corresponds with the purview of the Statute of Uses, 27th Henry VIII., c. 10.

POSTHUMUS. "Let there be *covenants* drawn between us."

IACHIMO. "Your hand; a *covenant.* We will have these things set down by lawful counsel, and straight away for Britain, lest the bargain catch cold, and starve; I will fetch my gold, and have our two wagers recorded."

Cymbeline, Act 1, *Scene* 5.

The covenants Shakespeare refers to in these passages are, according to the quaint description of Thomas Wood, (Institute of the Laws of England, 2nd ed., p. 228,) "agreements made by deed in writing, by the consent of two or more, to do, or not to do," and not the covenants *(conventiones,)* which are clauses of agreement contained in a deed.

BOLINGBROKE. "My heart this *covenant* makes, my hand thus *seals* it." *Richard II., Act* 2, *Scene* 3.

Covenants by deed *poll* are as effectual as those made by deed indented, if the party hath the deed to show. (1 Roll. abr., 517; Wood's Inst., 2nd ed., p. 230.) Bolingbroke seems to refer to a covenant by deed poll.

POSTHUMUS. "I embrace this condition; let us have *articles* betwixt us." *Cymbeline, Act* 1, *Scene* 5.

There may be *articles* of agreement, or covenants, framed according to the case, by mutual and reciprocal covenants, only to be performed by the parties, and this is good, if in writing and sealed and delivered by the parties, without the other formal parts of the deed.—Wood's Inst., 2nd ed., p. 230.

BUCKINGHAM. "The law I bear no malice for my death,
It hath done, upon the *premises*, but justice."
Henry VIII., Act 2, *Scene* 1.

Premises in law signify that part or beginning of a deed the office of which is to express the grantor, and grantee, and the land or thing granted or conveyed: and also the houses, lands, or places, &c., mentioned before.

PROSPERO. "Now the condition.
This King of Naples, being an enemy
To me inveterate, hearkens to my brother's suit;
Which was that he, in lieu o' the *premises*,
Of *homage*, and I know not how much tribute,
Should presently extirpate me and mine
Out of the kingdom."
Tempest, Act 1, *Scene* 2.

The premises of homage, the circumstances of homage mentioned before.

"Homage is the most honourable service, and most humble service of reverence, that a frank tenant may do to his lord. For when the tenant shall make homage to his lord, he shall be ungirt, and his head uncovered, and his lord shall sit, and the tenant shall kneel before him on both his knees, and hold his hands jointly together between the hands of his lord, and shall say thus: I become your man from this day forward, and unto you shall be true and faithful, and bear to you faith for the tenements that I claim to hold of you, saving the faith that I owe unto our Sovereign Lord the King; and then the lord, so sitting, shall kiss him."—Litt. s. 85.

VALENTINE. "This is the gentleman I told your ladyship
Had come along with me, but that his mistress
Did hold his eyes lock'd in her crystal looks.

SILVIA. "Belike, that now she hath *enfranchis'd* them
Upon some other pawn for *fealty*."

Act 2, *Scene* 5.

"Fealty is the same that *fidelitas* is in Latin. And when a freeholder doth fealty to his lord, he shall hold his right hand upon a book, and shall say thus: Know ye this, my lord, that I shall be faithful and true unto you, and faith to you shall bear for the lands which I claim to hold of you, and that I shall lawfully do to you the customs and services which I ought to do, at the terms assigned, so help me God and his saints; and he shall kiss the book. But he shall not kneel when he maketh fealty, nor shall he make such humble reverence as is aforesaid in homage."—Litt. s. 91.

CADE. "Men shall hold of me *in capite*."

Second Part Henry VI., *Act* 4, *Scene* 7.

Where the tenure was of the Sovereign, immediately it was said to be *in capite*, or in chief.

COUNTESS. "In delivering my son from me, I bury a second husband."

BERTRAM. "And I, in going, madam, weep o'er my father's death anew: but I must attend his Majesty's command, to whom I am now in *ward*, evermore in subjection."

All's Well That Ends Well, *Act* 1, *Scene* 1.

Tenure by homage, fealty, and escuage, is to hold by knight service, and it draweth to it *ward*, marriage, and relief. "For when such tenant dieth, and his heir male be within the age of twenty-one years, the lord shall have the land holden of him until the age of the heir of twenty-one years; the which is called full age, because such heir, by intendment of the law, is not able to do such knight's service before his age of twenty-one years. And, also, if such heir be not married at the time of the death of his ancestor, then the lord shall have the *wardship* and marriage of him."—Litt. s. 103. Wardship was abolished by the 12th Char. II., cap. 24.

PISANIO. "O! damn'd paper!
Black as the ink that's on thee! senseless bauble,
Art thou a *feodary* for this act, and look'st
So virgin like without?"
Cymbeline, Act 3, Scene 2.

Feodary was an ancient officer in the Court of Wards, (which was not instituted until 32nd Henry VIII., cap. 46, 33rd Henry VIII., cap. 22,) who was appointed by the master of that court, to be present with the escheator in every county at the finding of offices of lands; and to give evidence for the crown as well as for the value of the tenure; and his office was also to survey the lands of the ward after the office found, and to rate the value thereof into court; and likewise to assign dower to the king's widow, and to receive the rents of wards lands within his circuit, for which he was answerable to the receiver of the court. It seems to be used by Shakespeare in this passage in the sense of confederate, or associate.

YORK. "Seek you to seize and gripe into your hands
The royalties and rights of banish'd Hereford?
Is not Gaunt dead? and doth not Hereford live?
Was not Gaunt just? and is not Harry true?
Did not the one deserve to have an heir?
Is not his heir a well-deserving son?
Take Hereford's rights away, and take from time
His *charters* and his *customary rights*;
Let not to-morrow, then, ensue to-day;
Be not thyself, for how art thou a king,
But by fair sequence and sucession?
Now, afore God, (God forbid, I say true,)
If you do wrongfully seize Hereford's rights,

Call in the *letters patent* that he hath
By his *attornies-general* to *sue*
His livery, and deny his offer'd *homage*,
You lose a thousand well-disposed hearts,
And prick my tender patience to those thoughts
Which honour and allegiance cannot think.

KING RICHARD. "Think what you will, we seize into our hands
His plate, his goods, his money, and his lands."

King Richard II., Act 2, Scene 1.

When the male heir arrived to the age of twenty-one, or the heir female to that of sixteeen, they might *sue out their livery*, or *ousterlemain*, (Co. Litt. 77A.,) that is the delivery of their hands out of their guardian's hands. For this they were obliged to pay a fine, namely, half-a-year's profits of the land. An attorney is either *general* or special. A general attorney is he that is appointed by a general authority to manage all affairs or suits, as the *Attorney-General* of the king, who is usually one of the most learned of the barristers. He and the *Solicitor-General* are made by *letters patent, Quam diu se bene gesserint.*—(Terms of the Law, v. Attorney, 4 Inst. 117. Vent. 1. Wood's Inst., 2nd edition, p. 449.) Bolingbroke had appointed attornies to execute this office for him, if his father died during his banishment.

KING RICHARD. "Be the *attorney* of my love to her;
Plead what I will be, not what I have been."

Richard III., Act 4, Scene 4.

STANLEY. "I, by *attorney*, bless thee from thy mother."

Richard III., Act 5, Scene 3.

DUKE. "Not changing heart with habit, I am still
Attorney'd at your service."

Measure for Measure, Act 5, Scene 1.

CLOWN. "As fit as ten groats for the hand of an attorney.

All's Well That Ends Well, Act 2, Scene 3.

"Why should calamity be full of words?
Windy *attorneys* to their client's woes."

Richard III.

"But when the heart's *attorney* once is mute,
The *client* breaks, as desperate in his *suit*."

Venus and Adonis.

The heart's *attorney*, the heart's *tongue*.

DESDEMONA. "For thy *solicitor* shall rather die
Than give thy cause away."

Othello, Act 3, *Scene* 3.

HOTSPUR. "To *sue his livery* and *beg his peace*.

First Part, Henry IV, Act 4, *Scene* 3.

BOLINGBROKE. "I am denied to *sue my livery here*,
And yet my *letters patent* give me leave:
My father's goods are *all distrain'd* and sold,
And these, and all, are all amiss employ'd.
What would you have me do? I am a subject,
And challenge law. Attorneys are denied me,
And, therefore, personally I lay my claim
To my inheritance of free descent."

King Richard II., Act 2, *Scene* 3.

Royal grants, whether of lands, honours, liberties, franchises, or aught besides, are contained in *charters*, or *letters patent*, that is, open letters, *literæ patentes;* so called because they are not sealed up, but exposed to open view, with the great seal pendant at the bottom, and are usually directed or addressed by the sovereign to all subjects of the realm. And therein they differ from certain other letters of the sovereign, sealed also with his great seal, but directed to particular persons, and for particular purposes; which, therefore, not being proper for public inspection, are closed up and sealed on the outside, and are thereupon called writs close, *literæ clausæ*, and are recorded in the *close rolls*, in the same manner as the others are in the *patent rolls.*—Black Com. As to exemplification of letters patent see 3d and 4th Edw. VI., c. 4; 13th Elizabeth, c. 6.

"Set thy *seal manual* on my wax red lips."

Venus and Adonis.

Grants or letters patent must pass by *bill*, which is prepared by the Attorney and Solicitor General, in consequence of a warrant from the Crown, and is then signed, that is, superscribed at the top with the sovereign's own *sign manual*, and sealed with the privy signet, which is always in the custody of the principal Secretary of State; and then sometimes it immediately passes under the great seal, in which case the patent is subscribed in these words, "*per ipsam reginam*," by the Queen herself.—2 Rep. 17 b. Black Com.

CADE. "Is not this a lamentable thing, that of the skin of an innocent lamb should be made parchment? that parchment, being scribbled o'er, should undo a man? Some say, the bee stings; but I say, 'tis the *bee's wax*, for I did but seal once to a thing, and I was never mine own man since."

Second Part Henry VI., Act 4, Scene 2.

HAMLET. "How in my words soever she be shent,
To give them *seals* never, my soul, consent."

Act 3, Scene 2.

"What *wax* so frozen but dissolves with tempering,
And yields at last to every light impression."

Venus and Adonis.

The soft wax attached to a legal instrument upon which the seal was impressed, required to be tempered before the impression was made upon it, so Falstaff says:

"I have him already *tempering* between my finger and my thumb, and shortly will I *seal* with him."

KING. "Now must your conscience my acquittance *seal*."

Hamlet, Act 4, Scene 7.

IMOGEN. "Good wax, thy leave:
Blest the *bees* that make these locks of counsel;
Lovers and men in dangerous *bonds*, pray not alike;
Though *forfeiters* you cast in prison, yet
You clasp young Cupid's tables."

Cymbeline, Act 3, Scene 2.

The forfeitors had sealed to dangerous bonds; and in those times the seal was as binding as the signature, if not more so.

ANTONY. "Seal then and all is done."

Antony and Cleopatra, Act 4, Scene 12.

The neglect of signing, and resting only upon the authenticity of seals, remained very long among us, for it was held in all our books that sealing alone was sufficient to authenticate a deed; and so the common form of attestating deeds, "sealed and delivered," continues to this day.

"But my kisses bring again
SEALS of love but *sealed* in vain." *Song.*

HAMLET. "A combination and a form, indeed,
Where every god did seem to set his *seal*,
To give the world assurance of a man."

Act 3, Scene 4.

They seemed to give the world assurance of a man, in the most solemn form, that was, by setting their seals.

"Poor soul, the centre of my sinful earth,
Fool'd by those rebel powers that thee array,
Why dost thou pine within, and suffer dearth,
Painting thy outward walls so costly gay?
Why so large cost, having so short a *lease*,
Dost thou upon thy fading mansion spend?
Shall worms, *inheritors* of this excess,
Eat up thy charge? Is this the body's end?
Then, soul, live thou upon thy servant's loss,

And let that pine to aggravate thy store
Buy *terms* divine, in selling hours of dross;
Within be fed, without be rich no more:
So shalt thou feed on death, that feeds on men,
And, death, once dead, there's no more dying then.

Sonnet cxlvi.

A lease (from *laisser, dimittere*, to part with) is a demise or letting of lands, tenements, or hereditaments unto another for term of life, or years, or at will, upon a reserved rent, but always for a less time than the lessor hath in the premises; for, if it be for the whole interest, it is more properly an assignment than a lease.

MACBETH. "Rebellious head, rise never, till the wood
Of Birnam rise, and our high-placed Macbeth
Shall live the *lease* of *nature*, pay his breath
To time and mortal custom."

Act 4, *Scene* 1.

"The lease of nature," lease for term of life. Every one which hath an estate in any lands or tenements for term of his own or another man's life *(pur untre vie)* is called tenant of freehold, and none other of a lesser estate can have a freehold; but they of a greater estate have a freehold, for he in fee-simple hath a freehold, and tenant in tail hath a freehold, &c.—Litt. s. 57.

CADE. "These five days have I hid me in these woods, and durst not peep out, for all the country is lay'd for me; but now am I so hungry that, if I might have a lease of my life for a thousand years, I could stay no longer."

Tenant for term of years is where a man letteth lands or tenements to another for term of *certain* years after the number of years that is accorded between the lessor and the lessee. (Litt., s. 58.) Therefore, an estate of freehold, *liberum tenementum*, is an interest in lands, or other property, held by a *free tenure* for the life of the tenant, or that of some other person, for some *uncertain* term; (*Vide* Britt., c. 32; St. Germyn, D. & S. b. 2, d. 22;) but an estate *for a thousand years*, being for a certain term, is not a freehold, but only a *chattel*, and considered part of the personal estate.—*Vide* Co. Litt., 45, 46.

GHOST. "I am thy father's spirit;
Doom'd for a *certain term* to walk the night;
And, for the day, confined to fast in fires,
Till the foul crimes, done in my days of nature,
Are burn'd and purg'd away."

"Not mine own fears, nor the prophetic soul
Of the wide world dreaming on things to come,
Can yet the *lease* of my true love control,
Suppos'd as forfeit to a confin'd doom."

Sonnet cvii.

From these explanations the reader may perceive that Shakespeare does not confound a freehold estate with an estate less than freehold: for Cade does not mean to say "if I might have a lease for life, (which is an uncertain term, or freehold estate,) for a term of a thousand years, (which is a certain term or estate less than freehold,) but "if I might have a lease *of my life*, as I might have a lease *of a tenement for a thousand years*, I could stay no longer." But a lease for twenty or more years, *if* J. S. shall so long live, or *if* he should so long continue parson, is good: for there is a certain period fixed, beyond which it cannot last; though it may determine sooner, on the death of J. S. or his ceasing to be parson.—Co. Litt., 45.

THURIO. "What says she to my birth?"
PROTEUS. "That you are well deriv'd."
JULIA. "True, from a gentleman to a fool." [ASIDE.
THURIO. "Considers she my *possessions*?"

PROTEUS. "O, ay; and pities them."
THURIO. "Wherefore?"
JULIA. "That such an ass should own them." [ASIDE.
PROTEUS. "That they are out by *lease*."

Two Gentlemen of Verona, Act 5, Scene 2.

By his possessions *Thurio* means his hereditaments. *Proteus* alludes to his faculties, which he says are out by lease.

"It fears not policy, that heretic,
Which works on *leases* of short-number'd hours."

Sonnet cxxiv.

"Have I not seen dwellers on form and favour
Lose all and all by paying too much *rent*."

PRINCE HENRY. "Five years! by 'r lady, a long *lease* for the clinking of pewter. But, Francis, darest thou be so valiant as to play the coward with thy *indenture*, and to show it a fair pair of heels, and run from it."

First Part Henry IV., Act 2, Scene 4.

"To what state, what dignity, what honour,
Canst thou *demise* to any child of mine?"

Richard III.

The usual words of operation in a lease are ("demisi concessi et ad firmam tradidi,") "demise, grant, and to farm let."—Co. Litt., 45 b.; Wood's Inst., 2nd ed., p. 264.

1. GENTLEMAN. "I'll tell you in a little. The great duke
Came to the bar; where, to his accusations,
He *pleaded* still, *not guilty*, and alleged
Many sharp reasons to defeat the law.
The king's attorney, on the contrary,
Urg'd on the examinations, proofs, confessions
Of divers witnesses; which the duke desir'd
To him brought, *vivâ voce*, to his face."

Henry VIII., Act 2, Scene 1.

"Since brass, nor stone, nor earth, nor boundless sea,
But sad mortality o'er sways their power,
How with this rage shall beauty *hold a plea*,
Whose *action* is no stronger than a flower."

Sonnet lxv.

The liberty *to hold pleas* (tenere placita) is to have a court of one's own, and to hold it before a mayor, bailiff, &c., in such a place according to the course of the common law.—(C. Finch, 166, 1 Inst., 114 b., 2 Inst., 71, 4 Inst., 87, 224, 2 Danv. abr., 161.)

BASSANIO. "In law, what *plea* so tainted and corrupt
But, being seasoned with a gracious voice,
Obscures the show of evil."

Plea denotes what either party in a court alleges in a cause depending there; and plea or pleading, in a more extensive sense, comprehends all the points or matters that follow the declaration, both on the defendant's and plaintiffs side, till issue be joined; though a plea in its ordinary acceptation signifies the defendant's answer to the plaintiff's declaration.

TIMON. "Crack the *lawyer's* voice
That he may never more false title *plead,*
Nor sound his *quillets* shrilly."

Timon of Athens, Act 4, Scene 3.

HOLOFERNES. "Most barbarous intimation! yet a kind of insinuation, as it were, *in via*, in way of explication; *facere*, as it were *replication*."

Love's Labour Lost, Act 4, Scene 2.

HAMLET. "What replication should be made by the son of a king?"

Replication (replication) is an exception of the second degree made by the plaintiff upon the answer of the defendant.

DON JOHN. "Grow this to what adverse *issue* it can, I will put it in practice. Be cunning in the working this, and thy fee is a thousand ducats."

Much Ado About Nothing, Act 2, Scene 2.

When the parties by plea, replication, rejoinder, &c., are come to something affirmed by one, and denied by the other, they are at *issue*. Issue (from issuer, emanare, to flow, exitus) is a single certain and material point issuing out of the allegations and pleas of the plaintiff and defendant, consisting regularly of an affirmative and negative, to be tried by twelve men.—1 Inst., 126 a 11, Rep. 10, Finch, Book 4, ch. 35.

"Mine eye and heart are at a mortal war,
  How to divide the conquest of the sight;
Mine eye my heart thy picture's sight would bar,
  My heart mine eye the freedom of that right.
My heart doth *plead* that thou in him dost lie,
  (A closet never pierc'd with crystal eyes,)
But the defendant doth that plea deny,
  And says in him thy fair appearance lies.
To 'cide this title is impanelled
  A quest of thoughts, all tenants to the heart;
And by their verdict is determined
  The clear eye's *moiety*, and the dear heart's part:
As thus; mine eye's due is thine outward part,
  And my heart's right, thine inward love of heart.

Sonnet xlvi.

'To 'cide,' to decide. 'A quest of thoughts,' an inquest or jury. The process to bring in the jury in the Common Pleas is by venire facias and Habeas Corpora Juratorum. A Distringas juratorum goes out of the King's Bench to the same intent. Upon this writ of venire the sheriff shall return a jury in a *panel*, a little piece of parchment, annexed to the writ; on which account the jury is said to be *impanelled*.—Wood's Inst., 2nd ed., p. 590.

HAMLET. "For who would bear the whips and scorns of time,
The oppressor's wrong, the proud man's contumely,
The pangs of despised love, the law's delay,
The insolence of office, and the spurns

That patient merit from the unworthy takes,
When he himself might his *quietus* make
With a bare bodkin."

Act 3, *Scene* 1.

Quietus, is the same as to say freed or acquitted, and is used by the Clerk of the Pipe, and auditors in the Exchequer, in their discharges given to the accountants, which usually conclude with these words, *Abinde recessit quietus*, generally termed a *Quietus est*. There is a Roll in the Exchequer called the Pipe, otherwise the Great Roll. The Clerk of the Pipe is one in whose custody are conveyed, out of the offices of the King's and Treasurer's Remembrances, &c., (as water through a pipe into a cistern,) all accounts and debts due to the king; so as whatsoever is in charge in this Roll, or Pipe, is said in the law to be duly charged. (See Cowel's Interpreter *v.* Clerk of the Pipe.) The Controller of the Pipe is the Chancellor of the Exchequer.—Wood's Inst., 2nd edition, p. 470.

DAVY. "Those precepts cannot be served."

Henry IV., Act 5, *Scene* 1.

Precepts here signify commandments, in writing, issued out by a justice of the peace, &c., for bringing a person or records before him.

FALSTAFF. "Was it for me to kill the *heir apparent*.

Merry Wives of Windsor, Act 2, *Scene* 4.

Heirs apparent are such whose right of inheritance is indefeasible, provided they outlive the ancestor; as the eldest son, who must by the course of the common law be heir apparent to the father whenever he happens to die; and Falstaff refers to Prince Henry, who was the heir apparent to the king, his father.

FALSTAFF. "Go, hang thyself in thine own *heir apparent garters*."

First Part Henry IV., Act 2, *Scene* 2.

CLEON. "One sorrow never comes, but brings an *heir*,
That may succeed as his *inheritor*."
Pericles, Prince of Tyre, Act 1, *Scene* 4.

KING. "When sorrows come they come not single spies,
But in battalions!"
Hamlet, Act 4, *Scene* 5.

HASTINGS. "To bar my master's *heirs* in true descent."
Richard III., Act 3, *Scene* 2.

"So now I have confess'd that he is thine,
And I myself am *mortgag'd* to thy will;
Myself I'll forfeit, so that other mine
Thou wilt restore, to be my comfort still:
But thou wilt not, nor he will not be free,
For thou art covetous, and he is kind;
He learn'd but, *surety*-like, to write for me,
Under that *bond* that him as fast doth bind.
The *statute* of thy beauty thou wilt take,
Thou usurer, that putt'st forth all to use,
And sue a friend, came debtor for my sake;
So him I lose through my unkind abuse.
Him have I lost; thou hast both him and me;
He pays the whole, and yet am I not free.
Sonnet cxxxiv.

"The *statute* of thy beauty," "The bond or obligation of thy beauty." Statutes merchant and statutes staple have been explained.

LADY MACBETH. "What need we fear who knows it, when none can call our power to account."
Act 5, *Scene* 1.

LEAR. "No, they cannot touch me for coining;
I am the king himself."
King Lear, Act 4, *Scene* 6.

GONERIL. "Say, if I do; the laws are mine, not thine;
Who shall arraign me for 't."
King Lear, Act 5, *Scene* 3.

Lady Macbeth, Lear, and Goneril seem to refer to the ancient and fundamental principal of the English Constitution, that the king can do no wrong. *Rex non potest peccare.*—2 Roll. R. 304; Jenk. Cent. 9, 308.

EGEUS. "I beg the ancient privilege of Athens.
As she is mine, I may dispose of her,
Which shall be either to this gentleman
Or to her death; according to our law,
Immediately *provided in that case.*"

Midsummer Night's Dream, Act 1, *Scene* 1.

CADE. "*Contrary to the king, his crown, and dignity.*"

Henry VI., Act 4, *Scene* 6.

"Contrary to the form of the statute in that case made and provided" is the allegation which concludes indictments for offences which are contrary to the statute; if the offence is indictable at common law, the concluding words are, "against the peace of our said lady the Queen, her crown, and dignity."

CADE. "All the realm shall be *in common.*"

Second Part Henry VI., Act 4, *Scene* 2.

CADE. "Henceforward all things shall be *in common.*"

Second Part Henry VI., Act 4, *Scene* 7.

KING. "Leartes, I must common with your grief,
Or you deny me *right.*"

Hamlet, Act 4, *Scene* 5.

MARIA. "My lips are no *common* though *several* they be."

Love's Labour Lost, Act 1, *Scene* 1.

A common is unapportioned land; a several, land or an estate in severalty, is where an estate is held by one person in his own exclusive *right*, without any other person being interested therein. But *several*, or severell, in Shakespeare's native county, Warwick, signified, it is said, the *common field*, common to a few proprietors, but not common to all; so that the term used or taken in this sense would prevent the "though" appearing contradictory. Moreover, in Sonnet cxxxvii., Shakespeare seems to have been well aware of the distinction existing between these terms, for he there uses the word *several* in its usual legal acceptation :

"Why should my heart think that a *several* plot,
Which my heart knows the world's wide *common* place."

COSTARD. "The matter is to me, sir, as concerning Jaquenetta. The manner of it is, I was *taken with the manner*.

BIRON. "In what manner.

COSTARD. "In manner and form following."

Love's Labour Lost, Act 1, Scene 1.

PRINCE HENRY. "O villain, thou stolest a cup of sack eighteen years ago, and wert *taken with the manner*, and ever since thou hast blushed extempore."

First Part of King Henry IV., Act 2, Scene 4.

CLOWN. "If you had not *taken yourself with the manner*."

Winter's Tale, Act 4, Scene 3.

Mainour, old French *manoevre, meinor*, Latin *a manu*, from the hand, or in the work. The old law phrase, *to be taken as a thief with the mainour*, signifies to be taken in the very act of killing venison, or stealing wood, or in preparing so to do; or it denotes the being taken with the thing stolen in his hands or possession.

AARON. "He, that had wit, would think that I had none,
To bury so much gold under a tree,
And never after to inherit it."

In this passage Shakespeare probably refers to treasure trove (tresor trouve) treasure found, which signifies in our common law, as it does in the civil law, *id est veterem depositionem pecuniæ, cujus non extat memoria, ut jam dominium non habeat.* This treasure found, though the law gives it to the finder according to the law of nature, yet the law of England gives it to the crown by prerogative, if the owner be unknown.

THALIARD. "If a king bid a man be a villain, he is bound by the *indenture* of his oath to be one."

Pericles, Prince of Tyre, Act 1, *Scene* 2.

MARINA. "Serve by *indenture* to the common hangman.

Pericles, Prince of Tyre, Act 4, *Scene* 6.

LEAR. "This is nothing, fool.

FOOL. "Then 'tis like the breath of an unfeed lawyer."

Act 1, *Scene* 4.

IAGO. "And, in conclusion, *nonsuits*
My mediators."

A *nonsuit* (from the Norman-French *ne suit pas*) is when the plaintiff upon demand should appear in court, and he makes default by not prosecuting his suit with effect, or else by refusing to stand a verdict upon trial.—Wood's Inst., 2nd edition, p. 583.

"But be contented, when that fell *arrest*
Without all *bail* shall carry me away."

Sonnet.

HAMLET. "As this fell *sergeant* death is strict in his arrest."

Act 5, *Scene* 2.

Serjeant, or sergeant, is applied to divers offices and callings; but *Hamlet* refers to *serjeant-at-arms* or *mace*, whose office is to attend the king's person, to arrest traitors or persons of condition, and to attend the lord and high steward, when sitting in judgment.

DROMIO OF EPHESUS. "That you beat me at the mart, I have your hand to show.
If the skin were *parchment*, and the blows you gave were ink,
Your own handwriting would tell you what I think."

HAMLET. "Is not parchment made of sheepskins?

HORATIO. "Ay, my lord, and of calves' skins, too.

HAMLET. "They are sheep, and calves which seek out *assurance* in that."

Act 5, Scene 1.

"They are (the players) the *abstract* and brief chronicles of the time." *Hamlet, Act 2, Scene 2.*

"He hath an *abstract* for the remembrance of such places."

Merry Wives of Windsor, Act 4, Scene 2.

PAULINA. "The child was prisoner to the womb; and is,
By *law and process* of great nature, thence
Freed and *enfranchis'd*."

Winter's Tale, Act 2, Scene 2.

"*Pray in aid* for kindness."

Antony and Cleopatra.

Aid prier, to pray or crave assistance; and is a word used in pleading, for a petition to call in help from another person that has interest in land, or other thing contested. Aid of the king is where the king's tenant prays aid of the king on account of rent demanded of others. The aid of the king may be prayed by a city or borough that holds a fee-farm of the king where anything is demanded of them that belongs thereto.

"PANDARUS. "How now, a kiss in *fee-farm*."

Troilus and Cressida, Act 3, Scene 3.

Fee-farm is where a tenant holds of his lord in fee, paying annually the value, at least of a fourth part of the land, without homage, fealty, or other services to be done, more than are especially comprised in the feoffment.

FALSTAFF. "I will devise matter enough out of this Shallow to keep Prince Harry in continual laughter, the wearing out of six fashions, (which is four terms, or two actions,) and he shall laugh without *intervallums*."

King Henry IV., Part 2, Act 5, Scene 1.

Formerly the law terms regulated what is now called the season.

ORLANDO. "Who stays it (time) withal?

ROSALIND. "With *lawyers* in the vacation; for they sleep between term and term, and then they perceive not how time moves."

As You Like It, Act 3, *Scene* 2.

OLIVIA. "Let thy fair wisdom, not thy passion, sway
In this uncivil and unjust *extent*
Against thy peace;

Twelfth Night, Act 4, *Scene* 1.

DUKE F. And let my officers of such a nature
Make an *extent* upon his house and lands."

As You Like It.

Extent is directed to the sheriff to seize and value lands and goods to the utmost *extent*. The execution upon a *statute* or recognizance, pursuant to the 23rd Henry VIII., c. 6, is called an extent.—Wood's Inst., 2nd edition, p. 287, 566.

HOSTESS. "Master Fang, have you entered the action?

FANG. "It is entered.

HOSTESS. "I pray ye, since my exion is entered, and my case so openly known to the world, let him be brought in to his answer."

Henry IV., Act 2, *Scene* 1.

"Humbly complaining to your highness."

King Richard III.

Bills in Chancery commence "Humbly complaining to your lordship," &c.

YORK. "This is the day appointed for the *combat*,
And ready are the *appellant* and *defendant*."

Second Part Henry VI., Act 2, *Scene* 3.

Combat, in our ancient law, denoted a formal trial of a doubtful cause or quarrel by the swords or bastons of two champions. There was a trial by combat in the sixth year of the reign of King Charles I., between two Scotchmen,

Donald Rey, appellant, and David Ramsay, Esq., defendant; but, after many formalities, the matter was referred to the king's pleasure.

ARCITE. "I've a good title,
I am persuaded: this question, sick between us,
By bleeding must be cur'd. I am a suitor
That to your sword you will *bequeath* this *plea*,
And talk of it no more."

The Two Noble Kinsmen, Act 3, *Scene* 1.

FIRST SERVANT. "And say, you would present her at the leet,
Because he brought stone jugs and no *seal'd* quarts."

Taming the Shrew, Induc, Scene 2.

Sealed quarts, licensed quarts. At the court leet of a manor, the jury presented those who made use of false weights and measures.

FALSTAFF. "I say to you, I do desire deliverance from these officers, being upon hasty employment in the king's affairs."

Second Part King Henry IV., Act 2, *Scene* 1.

Protection, "cum clausula volumus," is an immunity given by the king to a person in his service to be free against suits at law for one year; and so from year to year. Thus, the king may grant a protection to his debtor that he be not sued till the king is paid his debt.—*Vide* 25th Edward III., c. 19, and Wood's Inst., 2nd edition, p. 571.

"I may be straight, though they themselves be bevel."

Sonnet cxxi.

An angle, except a right angle, is called a *bevel* angle, whether it be acute or obtuse. In deeds it is usual, in the description of property, to make use of the words "*bevelling line*" to signify the inclination of a surface from a right line.

ALCIABIADES. "I am a humble suitor to your virtues;
For pity is the virtue of the law,

And non but tyrants use it cruelly.
It pleases time and fortune to lie heavy
Upon a friend of mine, who, in hot blood,
Hath stepp'd into the law, which is past depth
To those that, without heed, do plunge into it."

Timon of Athens, Act 3, *Scene* 5.

KING. "Offence's gilded hand may shove by justice;
And oft 'tis seen the wicked prize itself
Buys out the law. But 'tis not so above:
There is no shuffling, there the *action lies*
In his true nature; and we ourselves compell'd,
Even to the teeth and forehead of our faults,
To give in evidence."

Hamlet, Act 3, *Scene* 3.

SECOND FISHERMAN. "Help, master, help; here's a fish hangs in the net, like a poor man's right in the law: it will hardly come out." *Pericles, Prince of Tyre, Act* 2, *Scene* 2.

The laws have been satirically compared to spiders' webs, which catch the small flies, and let the great ones through.

"I weep for thee, and yet no cause I have;
For why? Thou left'st me nothing in thy *will.*
And yet thou left'st me more than I did crave;
For why? I craved nothing of thee still:
O yes, dear friend, I pardon crave of thee;
Thy discontent thou didst *bequeath* to me."

The Passionate Pilgrim, 8.

"Poor deer," quoth he, "thou makest a *testament,* as worldlings do, giving thy sum of more to that which had too much."

As You Like It, Act 2, *Scene* 1.

VIOLA. "'Tis beauty truely blent, whose red and white
Nature's own sweet and cunning hand laid on:
Lady, you are the cruel'st she alive,
If you will lend these graces to the grave,
And leave the world no copy.

OLIVIA. "O, sir, I will not be so hard-hearted; I will give out divers schedules of my beauty. It shall be inventoried; and every particle and utensil labelled to my will: as, item, two lips indifferent red; item, two grey eyes, with lids to them; item, one neck, one chin, and so forth."

Twelfth Night; or, What You Will, Act 1, Scene 5.

Inventory is generally used to signify a *schedule*, containing a full description of all the goods and chattels of a testator at the time of his death, together with the value of the same, as apprised by two indifferent persons. (*Vide* 2nd Henry VIII., c. 5.) Viola by *copy* means issue; Olivia plays upon the word.

KING RICHARD. "Let's choose executors, and talk of wills;
And yet not so, for what can we *bequeath*,
Save our deposed *bodies to the ground*?.

Richard II., Act 3, Scene 2.

"This brief abridgment of my *will* I make:
My soul and body to the skies and ground."

The Rape of Lucrece.

The old forms of wills, commonly commenced by the testator commending his soul into the hands of God, his Creator, and his body to the earth, whereof it was made, Shakespeare's will commences in this manner:

"First, I commend my soul into the hands of God, my Creator, hoping and assuredly believing, through the only merits of Jesus Christ, my Saviour, to be made partaker of life everlasting, and my body to the earth whereof it is made."

"Thou, Collatine, shall *oversee* this will."

The Rape of Lucrece.

Old forms of wills often contained appointments of overseers, as well as executors.

"And so espous'd to death, with blood he *seal'd*
A testament of noble-ending love." *Henry V.*

SLENDER. "My *will?* Ods, heartlings, that's a pretty jest, indeed! I ne'er made my *will* yet. I thank heaven, I am not such a sickly creature; I give heaven praise."

Merry Wives of Windsor, Act 3, Scene 4.

ROMEO. "Bid a sick man in sadness make his *will:*
Ah! word ill urged to one that is so ill!

Romeo and Juliet, Act 1, *Scene* 1.

ELIZABETH. "Thou unadvised scold, I can produce
A *will* that *bars the title* of thy son."

King John, Act 2, *Scene* 1.

COUNT. "Of six preceding ancestors, that you
Conferr'd, by testament, to the *sequent issue,*
Hath been owed and worn."

All's Well That Ends Well, Act 5, *Scene* 3.

PAINTER. "To promise is most courtly and fashionable: performance is a kind of *will* or *testament* which argues a great sickness in his judgment that makes it."

Timon of Athens, Act 5, *Scene* 1.

The words *will* and *testament*, though generally used indiscriminately, are not, strictly speaking, synonymous. A will relates, properly, to real estate, and a testament to personal property requiring executors.

I have now quoted most of the passages in the works of William Shakespeare containing law terms, law customs, legal allusions, and legal phraseology, my memory has enabled me to refer to, excepting those which are incident to the plot of the play in which they occur, such as the passage in "Henry V.," act 5, scene 1, after the line, "In terram salicam mulieres ne succedant," that portion of scene 2, act 3, of "Julius Cæsar" referring to Cæsar's Will and Testament, and the Court of Justice scene, act 4 of the

"Merchant of Venice;" and although many of them would be unintelligible without sufficient explanation, excepting to those who have acquired a general knowledge of the various branches of the laws of England,—some of them have been afforded merely as examples of the frequent use the poet makes of the language of the law, though he may not always intend, in so doing, to convey a legal meaning.

Although ignorance of the theory and practice of the laws of England may have prevented many of Shakespeare's commentators from explaining or even perceiving the meaning of passages containing legal terms, &c., it will not account for the absurdity of some of their observations and emendatory criticisms. Persons of literary taste, familiar with the finest productions of the greatest authors of ancient and modern times, are not probably more grieved by the neglect of what is truly excellent in literature, and the preference given to the inferior writings of the day, than by the apparent incapacity of some men of acknowledged ability and profound learning to appreciate the fine touches of genius.

In the plays of Seneca, Corneille, and Dryden, when Jocasta discovers that Œdipus was the murderer of her husband, she continues to lament her affliction in the tedious and "set phrase of speech." But Shakespeare and Sophocles were poets of nature: in the Œdipus Tyrannus of Sophocles, Jocasta, after delivering the lines—

Ιοὺ, ἰοὺ, δύστηνε· τουτο γάρ σ' ἔχω
Μόνον προσειπεῖν, ἄλλο δ' οὔποθ' ὕστερον.

leaves the stage in the silence of her unutterable anguish; and Shakespeare frequently in one line, often even with a few words or short exclamations, expresses the most acute mental suffering.

LEAR. "O me, my heart! my rising heart; but down."

Act 2, Scene 3.

LEAR. "Wilt break my heart?"

Act 3, Scene 4.

After contemplating the misery of Edgar, Lear says:

"Thou wert better in thy grave than to answer with thy uncover'd body this extremity of the skies. Is man no more than this? Consider him well. Thou owest the worm no silk, the beast no hide, the sheep no wool, the cat no perfume: Ha! here's three of us are sophisticated! Thou art the thing itself: unaccomodated man is no more but such a poor, bare, forked animal as thou art. Off, off, you lendings: Come, *unbutton here*.

Act 3, Scene 4.

A commentator, in a note on this passage, observes, "The words *unbutton here* are probably only a marginal direction crept into the matter!" Shakespeare, however, makes use of the same expression in another part of King Lear.

LEAR. "Pray you, *undo this button*. Thank you, sir,
Do you see this! Look on her, look, her lips.
Look there, look there! [*Dies.*

Act 5, Scene 3.

Moreover, such expressions, intended to describe the anguish of the "o'er fraught heart," are not peculiar to this play.

QUEEN ELIZABETH. "Ah, cut my lace asunder,
That my pent heart may have some scope to beat,
Or else I swoon with this dead, killing news."

King Richard III., Act 4, Scene 1.

PAULINA. "Woe the while!
O, cut my lace, lest my heart, cracking it,
Break too!"
Winter's Tale, Act 3, Scene 2.

In the third scene of the first act of the "Merchant of Venice," Shylock says,

"Signior Antonio, *many a time and oft*
In the Rialto, you have rated me
About my monies and my usances."

The actor who first made this alteration,

"Signior Antonio, *many a time,—and oft*
In the Rialto, you have rated me
About my monies and my usances,"

was considered to have exercised much ingenuity, and his example has been very generally followed, both on and off the stage, it being stated that the expression "many a time and oft" is tautological, and could never have been intended by so great a master of the English language. Now, although in this passage the expression is so situated as to admit of a double reading, it is not certain that the poet intended such reading to be adopted; for, contrary to the statement generally made, that the expression is peculiar to the "Merchant of Venice," it occurs in several other portions of Shakespeare's works, where it is so situated as not to admit of such alteration:

FALSTAFF. "Well, thou has called her to a reckoning *many a time and oft.*"
First Part Henry IV., Act 1 Scene 2.

WIFE. "Most true, forsooth; and *many a time and oft* myself have heard a voice to call him so.
Second Part Henry VI., Act 2, Scene 1.

LUCULLUS. "*Many a time and oft* I have dined with him, and told him on't."

Timon of Athens, Act 2, Scene 1.

MARCELLUS. "Knew you not Pompey? *Many a time and oft*
Have you climb'd up to walls and battlements,
To towers and windows, yea, to chimney tops,
Your infants in your arms, and there have sat
The live long day, with patient expectation,
To see Great Pompey pass the streets of Rome;
And when you saw his chariot but appear,
Have you not made an universal shout,
That Tyber trembled underneath her banks
To hear the replication of your sounds,
Made in her concave shores?"

Julius Cæsar, Act 1, *Scene* 1.

To conclude, whether William Shakespeare was or was not a member of the legal profession, sufficient has probably been stated to prove that he had acquired a general knowledge of the laws of England,—the accumulated wisdom of ages, the stronghold of freedom, of civil and religious liberty,—the wisest, the noblest, the most fair and equitable system of jurisprudence ever respected and obeyed by the just, or calumniated and violated by the evil, or that the human race in any age or any clime has ever yet beheld!